Dan Kennedy's
Ordinary People, Extraordinary Entrepreneurs and Success Coaches

ISBN #0-9718653-0-2

TABLE OF CONTENTS

INTRODUCTION

At age 72, Arnold Palmer has retained the services of a "swing coach". He has helped Palmer change his stance, he has convinced Palmer to change clubs, he is working with Palmer to compensate for loss of flexibility and strength that inevitaby comes with his senior citizen status. This coach, 34-year-old Doug Mauch, the director of golf at The Tradition, has a 'system' for helping older golfers play to their potential. Arnold Palmer says he hasn't had a teacher or a coach since his father first taught him to play golf. Old dogs can learn new tricks.

Arnold Palmer is a rare bird. Most other pro golfers have coaches throughout their entire careers. Most pro athletes of every variety rely on coaches, some also on 'sports psychologists.'

Truth is, everybody needs a coach, a consultant, an advisor with specialized knowledge and experience, a pair of "fresh eyes" from time to time, if not continually, in order to achieve maximum success.

In this book, you will meet eight top consultants and coaches, in addition to me, each profiled in their own chapter. Each has a 'system for success' in their respective fields, tested and proven to such an extent, by so many people, it's fair to call it "fail-safe."

The line between 'coaching' and 'consulting' is blurry. There is one-on-one coaching, via telephone conversations or in-person sessions, but there is also group coaching, typically via teleconferences. Some coaching is directly linked to a particular system, and might be described as interactive teaching. Other coaching is totally individualistic, responsive to the person's needs, and is closer to therapy than teaching. Consulting is almost always one-on-one and may mimic coaching but also, usually, includes the consultant actively doing some of the work or providing other services to the client. Sometimes, the system is taught in seminars; coaching is in follow-up. In addition, there is the do-it-yourself variation, where teaching, tools and sometimes interactive work is provided in "box form", in books, manuals, cassettes, CD's, CD-ROM's and web sites, and in "continuity form"; those same kinds of materials delivered on a monthly or other scheduled, continuing basis. The objectives are the same: to teach a workable system, to enhance the ability of the client to use the system, to improve the results the client gets from the system.

Each of the people in this book teach a system or systems, or at least employ one as consultants. Most provide consulting, coaching, and "box" and "continuity" materials. The range of clientele they assist is incredibly diverse. One works with multi-million dollar investment firms, banks and real estate investors with global portfolios; another works with the average guy, investing in a single family home. Others serve niche industries, like carpet cleaning or auto repair.

One or maybe more than one of them might be just the coach you need, provide just the opportunity you're looking for - even if you didn't know you were looking for it before reading this book!

At the very least, you will find "clues" to achieving exceptional success in any edeavor throughout their stories.

It is my privilege to work with these fine people, and to introduce them to you.

Dan Kennedy
www.dankennedy.com

Chapter #1

The Unlikeliest Coach

<u>THERE MAY BE NO ONE ELSE LESS LIKELY TO BECOME A LEGENDARY SUCCESS COACH THAN JOE POLISH.</u>

I met Joe Polish 8 years ago, and I was immediately impressed with his unusual variation of the great American rags-to-riches, Horatio Alger story. Imagine a once dead-broke, markedly unsuccessful carpet cleaner being paid well over 6-million dollars by members of his own industry for his business advice. Unlikely? Certainly. But that is just one of the improbable realities about one of America's fastest rising success coaches, 34-year-old Joe Polish.

He is often underestimated. Until recently, he sported a long pony-tail, and looked more like a rock group's "roadie" than a business consultant. He is young. Brash. At times, horribly disorganized, an admitted procrastinator. He drives a Jaguar (given to him as a gift by a grateful client). As a speaker he is the anti-thesis of a precisely polished Tony Robbins. It would be easy to underestimate him. It would be a mistake.

His success story begins, as so many such stories do, with disadvantage, frustration and failure. At age 23, he was barely ekeing out a living as a carpet cleaner, living from job to job, and on credit cards in between, and wondering what else he might do. He asked a very successful businessman for advice on a different field to switch to, and the businessman let him have it. He asked Joe tough questions, told Joe about the size and magnitude of the opportunity in his present field, and suggested that if he switched businesses he would carry with him the same attitudes and behaviors that were holding him back where he was.

So Joe stuck.

After numerous frustrating attempts to follow the examples of carpet cleaning advertising he saw used by others, wasting money on an ad agency, and struggling mightily to conquer the challenge of how to create a steady flow of new customers, Joe discovered direct-response marketing. He found materials from a direct marketing guru named Gary Halbert. Gary's writings opened Joe's eyes to an entirely different way of thinking about advertising. They also led Joe to me. Joe got his hands on my materials, my 'Ultimate Sales Letter' book, my 'Magnetic Marketing System'. My materials led him to other direct-response marketing teachers. He immersed himself in all this and quickly emerged with entirely new strategies that revolutionized his business. At a rapid pace, Joe created unique recorded "consumer awareness" messages, a new way of selling services called a "Carpet Audit"™, "value packages" instead of just price quotes by the square foot, and direct-mail campaigns featuring gigantic photos of dust mites.

Before you could sneeze, Joe had his business humming.

Other carpet cleaners began nosing around, asking him how he was doing so well, making fumbling attempts at copying some of his advertising. I and others encouraged him to put everything he was using so successfully into a "kit" to sell to others in his industry. Ultimately, I wound up working with him personally on this project. What has transpired in the ensuing 7 years is nothing short of amazing.

Remarkable Dominance Of
The Cleaning Industry

There's over 16-billion square feet of carpeting manufactured and installed every year. Sooner or later, it must all be cleaned. Homes, apartment buildings, offices, stores, restaurants, country clubs, carpet, carpet everywhere. This makes the carpet cleaning business an evergreen, ever-growing industry, populated by every size operation, from homebased mom'n pops to large companies with dozens of trucks, even their own cleaning plants for rugs and draperies. Throughout this huge, diverse industry, no other advisor, trainer or consultant can come even close to Joe's impact and reach. Over 19,000 carpet cleaners world wide have attended Joe's seminars, presentations at industry conventions, or come to his company - Piranha Marketing ("Eat Your Competition Alive!")™ looking for business-building assistance. At the moment, there are over 3,600 cleaning company owners who are Piranha Marketing Members, using his basic business systems, over 250 owners in his on-going telecoaching program (at $247.00 a month), and in 2001, over 300 attended his annual "marketing boot camp" in Phoenix, each paying an average of $1,000.00 to be there, and some traveling from as far away as the United Kingdom and Australia to attend. In his new, high-level Platinum Plus Coaching Program, there are nearly 40 business owners, each paying $10,000.00 per year.

Controversy Follows
Joe Polish

In 1997, the then #1 industry trade journal, *CleanFax,* named him Industry Man Of The Year, and featured a cover photo of two Joes, back to back, one as the devil in red hood and cape with pitchfork, one as an angel with halo; a photographic nod to the controversy that surrounds him within his industry. In 1999 he assisted ABC-TV's 20/20 with an undercover "sting" operation, exposing fraudulent 'bait-n-switch' sales tactics commonly used in the carpet cleaning industry, and appeared in 20/20's program featuring an actual 'sting' recorded with hidden cameras. While many members of his industry applauded him, he also received negative, even threatening calls and letters. If you haunt industry web sites with "chat rooms" and open forums, you'll find Joe Polish a frequent topic of debate and argument, with his Members or "followers" touting their successful results from following his advice; with jealous competitors and a few disgruntled cleaners offended by him insisting he is a fraud. The natural question is: does this coach's coaching work?

Here is a telling fact: when a representative sampling of the 1999 and 2000 Marketing Boot Camp attendees were surveyed months and a year following their attendance, their average annual income increase proved to be $40,000.00. Joe tells cleaners: "If you consider yourself just average, then this proves applying my methods should be worth at least $40,000.00 to you the first year. If you happen to be above average, you should do even better."

What His Clients And Members Say

Here are two comments fairly representative of the hundreds on file in Joe's office:

"Thanks to Joe Polish, I increased my business by over $100,000.00 the first year I used his program. And with only one truck. Thanks again!"

> - Piranha member Robert Peters who makes over $325,000.00 per year with ONE truck.

"About 3 years ago I was near bankruptcy, my house had been foreclosed on, and I was going through a tough divorce and in the settlement, my ex-wife had taken the most profitable part of my business...then I heard about your marketing ideas in a trade journal. I decided to give your marketing program a try because of your incredible guarantee. I was so broke that I had to use your payment plan on my VISA.....Since becoming a Piranha Member, I have been able to enjoy the good life. In the first 6 months of being a Piranha Member, my girlfriend and I took our first vacation to La Jolla, California. Hey, it's not much, but it was all I could afford at the time. The following year, we went to Paris and London. Oh, and during those 2 years, I was able to remodel a bedroom and rebuild a bathroom and part of our roof on our home....Did I mention that I've only used about five of your ideas out of the hundreds you have to offer, and that I suffer from a severe negative personality trait? You see, I procrastinate. Thank you!"

- John Stewart, Healthy Choice Carpet Cleaners

Going Beyond
The Cleaning Industry

Today, Joe has branched out far afield from just the carpet cleaning industry, notably with his 'Genius Network' monthly series of audio cassettes and CD's featuring his exclusive interviews with an amazing array of famous authors and speakers, business leaders, and top experts in fields ranging from time management to selling. How does Joe get such a remarkable, ever-expanding list of celebrities and hugely successful entrepeneurs to be interviewed for his Genius Network? "I ask them," Joe says, "and there's a classic success principle demonstrated right there - ask for what you want."

Here is a partial list of Joe's interviews currently available on tapes from The Genius Network library:

- **Robert Kiyosaki,** author, RICH DAD, POOR DAD - on Creating Personal Wealth

- **Michael Gerber,** author, E-MYTH - on Systemizing Your Business

- **Dan Sullivan**, founder, 'Strategic Coach' - on How The Best Entrepreneurs Get Better

- **Ken Glickman**, from Boardroom Reports - on The Best Management System Ever

- **Mark Victor Hansen,** co-author, CHICKEN SOUP FOR THE SOUL

- **Barbara Hemphill,** author, TAMING THE PAPER TIGER

- **Denny Hatch**, founder, Target Marketing Magazine - on Million Dollar Marketing Secrets

- **Brian Holloway**, NFL champion, speaker - on Overcoming Obstacles

- **Joe Sugarman**, inventor of Blu-Blockers sunglasses™ - on Psychological Triggers In Selling

- **Dan Wheeler**, top on-air personality at QVC - on Creating The Perfect Selling Environment

- **Ken Kerr,** a former creative director at Epcot and Sea World - on The Marketing Secrets Of Disney

- **Brian Tracy**, famous speaker/author - on Strategies For Massive Success

(Complete list at www.thegeniusnetwork.com)

Many of these people have been interviewed countless times by journalists, radio and TV talk show hosts and others, yet say that Joe is the best interviewer they've ever encountered. This has led to Joe being hired to interview both celebrities and company owners, CEO's and entrepreneurs, in order to create unique "audio brochures" for them, as well as draw out of them ideas for their advertising and marketing messages. Joe charges between $3,000.00 and $6,000.00 to prepare for, and conduct such an interview for a client, and, depending on the situation, to edit the recording for audio brochure purposes, and to review its transcript with the client for other purposes. One such client has distributed over 15,000 copies of the resulting audio tape, and ranks it as his best prospecting tool ever. Incredibly, many of the people interviewed for Joe's Genius Network tapes have actually paid to be interviewed, and to have the use of that same tape for their own marketing purposes! Joe explains, "I have put together a business where I get paid by the person I interview, who, sometimes, I'd be excited about interviewing free, and I get to use the content in my product, which I get paid for again by all my Network subscribers. In this way, the two hours or so of my time invested in each interview is sometimes worth $20,000.00 to $25,000.00, and maybe that makes me one of the highest paid interviewers on the planet!"

Maybe if you broke down the salaries of Barbara Walters, Mike Wallace or Larry King per interview, they are paid more. But it is undoubtedly a very short list of interviewers getting paid so handsomely.

"The lesson in that", Joe says, " is leverage. Entrepreneurs, authors, everybody, needs to hunt for hidden or different or breakthrough ways they can leverage their time, and escape the dollars-per-hour norms of their industry, or of the world at large."

Unique Business-Building Processes

Another aspect of Joe's business is the development and sale or licensing of copyright, trademark and even patent protected processes for improving businesses of all kinds, in various ways. For example, there is his 'Piranha Marketing Money Map'™, a ten module blueprint for maximizing business profits.....the Prospect Conveyor Belt™, which includes automated advertising and marketing tools, such as 25 different recorded messages, consumer education guides, and powerful lead generation ads and flyers.....and the Business Bullseye™, for focusing and clarifying a business' advertising message. Companies frequently pay

$10,000.00 to as much as $50,000.00 to acquire and use these processes.

When asked about the pricey fees, Joe explains, "It is kind of amazing, isn't it, that a guy who was a carpet cleaner, pushing a cleaning wand, worrying about getting the next job before running out of money, now gets companies to fork over more money for one of his processes than he used to make all year. But here's the moral of that story: everything's about value, and discounting from value. In my business, in any business, there are no actual, fixed price ceilings, and price resistance from customers is a symptom of other flaws, not a reality itself. Everybody wants and responds to a bargain. Everybody buys what is a bargain to them. A $200.00 carpet cleaning job might be a bargain to one homeowner, depending on her economic status, the value of her home, the value to her of entertaining in her home, the guarantees offered by the cleaner, and so on, but a $200.00 price for a carpet cleaning job might be outrageous, even prohibitively expensive to that same homeowner if the proper value wasn't established. The same is true with my proprietary marketing processes. If a client sees that they are worth considerably more to him than they cost, the amount, the price itself doesn't matter. But even if sold at 99 cents, if the client can't see they are worth a lot more than that to him, he won't buy. The issue is discount from value, not price."

Never At Rest

Joe Polish is, at least at this stage in his life, never at rest, always starting yet another new service for his members, subscribers and clients, launching yet another new business, or birthing yet another new product. On the drawing board for 2002 - 2003: a new national trade magazine for the carpet cleaning industry.....a new coaching program "bundling" his proprietary processes with tele-coaching......and launch of a new line of cleaning products for homes, to be sold through carpet cleaners as well as direct to consumers, via home shopping TV.

CONTACT INFORMATION:

You can obtain more information about THE GENIUS NETWORK at www.TheGeniusNetwork.com or by FAXing a request for a tape catalog and subscription information to 480-858-0004. If you own or manage a company, and are interested in Joe's proprietary business development processes, private consulting, or having Joe speak for your organization, please call his office directly at 480-858-0008 or FAX to 480-858-0004 or visit www.joepolish.com.

If you own a carpet cleaning company or janitorial service, request a free copy of Joe's Special Report "How To Double Your Business...Even In A Tough Economy" by calling his office at 1-800-275-2643 or FAXing a request to 480-858-0004 or visiting www.joepolish.com.

Joe does not make his e-mail address public, but you can reach his staff at support@JoePolish.com.

* * * * * *

Chapter #2

A David Against Goliaths

Today's independent retailers often feel like they are in the fight of their lives, up against juggernauts ranging from Wal-Mart, the biggest behemoth of all, to superstores in each specialty category, like Home Depot and Lowes in hardware, Best Buy in electronics, Barnes&Noble in books, and so on.

In downtown Baltimore, there once were fourteen competing menswear stores, each independently and locally owned - just like in many large cities' downtowns. Over a handful of years, as suburban malls proliferated, and giant national chain stores entered the market, thirteen of those stores - some there for decades - closed their doors. The last store standing, Gage "World Class" Menswear, captained by Bill Glazer, has not only survived, it has prospered beyond any rational expectation. In fact, in recent years, while the entire menswear retailing industry has been in the doldrums, and independent stores everywhere have struggled just to stay even, Bill's downtown store as well as his suburban store, have enjoyed double-digit annual growth and per square foot profits roughly 250% better than the industry average. Maybe even more amazing, when the "Goliath" national discounter 'Mens Wearhouse' opened near Bill's stores and commenced a massive ad campaign, his sales still improved rather than suffered.

How can this be? What is Bill's secret?

The answer: Bill's strategies for prospering against all odds have made him something of a celebrity in his industry, and propelled him into a second business as top marketing and business consultant to over 500 other retail store owners nationwide. I added fuel to all that, as I began urging Bill to "package up" everything he was doing to promote his stores when I first met him in 1997.

As you might imagine, given my thousands of Inner Circle Members, extensive travels, speaking to over 200,000 businesspeople a year for ten consecutive years, I've seen the advertising and marketing of thousands of retailers. As I told Bill, I am happy to tell you: nobody, and I mean nobody has a handle on direct-response advertising and marketing for retail stores like Bill does.

Forget All About
'Normal' Retail Advertising

Bill probably spends less on advertising than most other stores his size, because he does such a phenomenal job of maximizing value from his own mailing list, which now tops 52,000. His 'Thanksgiving Card' mailing is so profitable and successful he has canned and cloned it, to sell to the 500 other retailers who are members of his Retail Marketing System.

But even farther outside the norms of marketing in retail are the ways he supports his ads and mailings with technology-based, automated marketing. For example, Bill frequently uses voice-broadcast blasts to call all his customers and leave messages on their answering machines or voice mail instantaneously. "For less than ten cents per person, I deliver a message in my voice, or using voice impersonators, have Elvis or former President Clinton deliver my message," Bill explains. "This has increased response to a mailing by as much as 92%."

Bill is also an adept event marketer. His semi-annual, off-premises 4-day sale at Maryland State Fairgrounds grows in size and fame year by year, most recently attracting over 10,000 customers!

Dragging An "Old" Industry Into
21st Century Direct Marketing

"The menswear industry is largely comprised of second, third, and even fourth generation family businesses both blessed and cursed with traditions," Bill says, "now up against the equivalent of Wal-Mart in big chains and discounters. The independent stores cannot compete on price, yet are woefully behind the times in use of smart marketing strategies, technology, and alternative media. The salvation and prosperity of my stores has been entirely due to my literally turning my back on the way retail stores have always advertised and operated, going outside the industry, and returning with direct marketing completely foreign to our business, but proven elsewhere."

Slowly, in some cases skeptically, and in some cases reluctantly, others in Bill's industry are coming around. In less than three years, over 500 store owners have purchased his marketing "kits," began using his ads and mailings, started using technology he's introduced to them like voice broadcast, and are achieving truly remarkable results. For example, a Texas store owner says he completely revamped his mailings due to Bill, and with one promotion did 6 months worth of business in 2 weeks! A Nebraska store owner with 25 years' experience hesitantly tried one of Bill's ideas and had a recordbreaking week of sales. There are hundreds of such success stories in Bill's files and on display (with full store names and locations) at his web site, billglazermarketing.com.

In 2000, the industry journal MR (Menswear Retailing) named Bill and his BGS Marketing System to the list of the top 100 people, places, and things notable in the industry for the new millenium......the equivalent of being named to *People* or *Time Magazine's* list of 100 most noteworthy or influential individuals. Bill also writes a monthly column on marketing for MR, and frequently redistributes a synopsis of these articles via his own *"FAX TIMES"* industry newsletter, reaching over 10,000 stores throughout North America.

Maybe more important than any specific promotion is the way Bill guides his clients to an entirely new and different way of thinking about their businesses. Randy Diamond of Diamonds Menswear stores, some of the oldest and most successful throughout northeastern Ohio, says: "I was brought up in the old school, that if you bought well, merchandised well, and had a good staff on the floor, business would increase. But we have found it difficult to get additional growth in recent years. Your focus on continuous, proactive marketing is key. This was a reorientation of my mindset. The results have been phenomenal."

"Menswear retailers, and retailers in all categories have been conditioned to focus on merchandising, staffing and newspaper or radio advertising. While all these things are important, they are no longer enough," Bill explains. "We work with a 12 month calendar of pre-planned and integrated ad campaigns, direct-mail campaigns, sales, seasonal events, and free gift promotions. We place more emphasis on marketing to our own list of past and present customers than on mass advertising. Being in the business of marketing your stores vs. operating your stores really is a distinctly different way of thinking."

In his role as these retailers' guide to the brave new world, Bill says he must coach them on new ways of thinking about the nature of their role in their business, their relationship with their customers, their competitive positioning, as well as the nuts-and-bolts of more effective advertising and profitable direct-mail. Perhaps the shining jewel of Bill's accomplishments was his winning of the prestigious RAC Award at the 2002 Retail Advertising Conference. This honor is equivalent in retail as the Oscars are to movies and the Emmys to television. Imagine an independent retailer competing and winning against giants like Target, Wal-Mart, Chevrolet, Best Buy and Payless Shoe Source.

Beyond Menswear: Bill Glazer Takes On The Entire Spectrum Of Retail

It seems that the independent and small-chain retailers in all product categories share common challenges with those in menswear, including their David vs. Goliath battles with "big box" superstores and discounters, increasing advertising clutter, and public resistance to traditional advertising. And it turns out that the solutions Bill has pioneered first with his stores, then with the more than 500 menswear store owners nationwide using his methods, are readily transferred to other types of retail.

Bill's first testing beyond his own industry was with retail stores selling outdoor equipment, camping goods, and sporting goods - and the first campaign he created for them generated an amazing 7-million dollars in sales from just $200,000.00 in marketing costs, in just 60 days. For an auto dealership, one of Bill's sales letters and a voice broadcast campaign created over $200,000.00 in sales, from a total expenditure of $557.00. Others enthusiastically embracing his systems include owners of hardware stores, home and garden centers, private postal centers, even dentists.

In 2000, Bill Glazer was selected as one of the two top businesspeople of the year for the state of Maryland by the U.S. Small Business Administration. Personally, I've probably featured samples of Bill's ads and direct-mail campaigns in my 'No B.S. Marketing Letter' more than samples from any other business owner or marketer. I would emphatically urge anyone in retail, whether the owner of a single store or the CEO of a chain, to get, study, and use Bill's marketing materials.

CONTACT INFORMATION:

BGS MARKETING
c/o Gage Menswear
200 W. Baltimore Street
Baltimore, MD 21201
Phone: 1-800-545-0414
FAX: 410-727-4174
E-mail: bg@gagemenswear.com

For individuals interested in purchasing Bill's marketing system kits, either for the menswear industry or general retail, or inquiring about consulting, coaching programs or having Bill speak to a group, you can call toll-free, 1-800-545-0414.

* * * * * *

Chapter #3

Revving Up Marketing For Auto Repair Shop Owners

Somewhat analogous to the retailers Bill Glazer assists, the nation's independent auto repair shop owners (as well as franchisees) operate in an advertising and marketing battle zone dominated by giant national chains with huge budgets for mass advertising, as well as car dealerships' service departments. Most car repair business owners are further handicapped by what Ron Ipach calls "the technical obsession"; a near myopic focus on, and love for doing the mechanical work, and only a grudging attention to marketing as a necessary evil. "Most repair shop owners were mechanics working for somebody else," Ron explains, "and they have a rough time shaking the worker mentality and adopting the entrepreneurial mindset."

Ron Ipach is coaching hundreds of such shop owners, to change their own attitudes, and to get passionately involved in marketing, just as he did.

From Near-Poverty To A 6-Figure Income In 18 Months

In 1994, Ron Ipach was in the windshield repair business, a one man show, operating out of the back of his pick-up truck, earning a mere $13,000.00, and struggling with the heavy burden of a very negative attitude about himself, his business and his future. "I suppose I was a typical blue collar guy in my kind of business," Ron says, "seeing myself as downtrodden, doing a lot of griping and complaining."

Oddly, the jumpstart in Ron's turnaround was a TV news report about a comatose woman in a nursing home, raped and impregnated while in a coma. "That horrible story made me decide to turn off the news for a while. I'd been kind of a news and talk radio junkie, but I realized that was mostly, only contributing to my unproductive attitude." At the public library, Ron picked up some audio cassettes featuring my speaking colleagues, Zig Ziglar (on motivation) and Tom Hopkins (on selling), and just listening to those tapes began affecting Ron's thinking, and also positively affecting his bank account. So, when he saw the big SUCCESS event advertised in his newspaper, featuring the speakers he'd been listening to on tape, as well as a dozen others, he bought a ticket and went to the all day event in Cincinnati, in 1995.

It was at that event that Ron heard me for the first time, bought a bundle of my tapes and materials, and added me to his list of "distance mentors." As he listened and learned, Ron quickly realized he'd been doing business just about devoid of any direct marketing, wasting money on copy-cat advertising doomed to fail or attract only bargain hunters, and he resolved to adapt the very different kinds of marketing strategies he'd discovered to his type of business - and the results were extraordinary. In just 18 short months, his income skyrocketed from $13,000.00 a year to nearly that much each month!

I asked if he thought such dramatic, to most, unbelievable income increases were possible for others, or whether he had benefited from some unique circumstances. "I'm convinced," Ron answered, "that virtually anybody struggling and barely making a living in that business (windshield repair) or in auto repair, anywhere in the country, could experience exactly the same kind of results I did - in fact, it's that conviction that led me to teaching and sharing my methods with others." Ron further points out that there was and is nothing unique about him: he grew up in Cincinnati, has a two year college education, and, after all, he was doing windshield repair work for his living - where, he asks rhetorically, is the unique and unduplicatable advantage there? And Ron's meteoric income increase was not the result of luck either. No big repair contract from one lucky contact. Nothing like that. Just infinitely smarter marketing to obtain good customers married with a fresh, optimistic, entrepreneurial attitude.

Now He Shows Thousands
How To Make As Much Money Each Month
As They've Been Making All Year

In November of 1996, Ron first took his most successful ads, flyers, sales letters, and strategies for pricing, "package selling", multiplying customers through formalized referral programs, and all his experience and put it into a "system" complete with manuals and audio tapes, and offered it to others in the windshield repair industry, then the auto glass business, and ultimately the entire auto repair industry. Today, his "Auto Repair Marketing Success System" has over 2,200 Members utilizing his methods, ranging from backyard-garage freelance mechanics and small repair shops to nationally franchised repair businesses and large independent garages. "One of my clients owns a car repair business doing over $3-million a year, and he's grown by 20% a year for each of the past two years." At the opposite end of the spectrum, another client took Ron's marketing ideas and multiplied his income by over five times:

"When I met Ron, I was a one man business renting a one bay 'hole-in-the-wall' garage. Thanks to Ron's marketing strategies I now own a large full service shop in the best corner of town. I can now spend time with my family and pursue other hobbies and dreams while my good crew runs the shop!"

- Rob Russell, Accurate Auto, Oregon

In addition to the marketing systems he's provided to the more than 2,200 business owners nationwide, Ron holds an annual "Marketing Boot Camp" attended by 70 to 100 owners - each paying $1,597.00 to be there - who are very serious about growing their businesses. He also offers an on-going telecoaching program. And Ron's most recent new product, a "Car Care Club Card" for consumers, is being sold by hundreds of repair shops and service stations.

"The Car Care Club Card is a package of discount coupons for goods and services every car owner needs. We customize the card for the repair shop, provide signage, window posters, a proven direct-mail program and other sales tools, and training, so that the owner winds up with a very significant new business within his business. This is a product consumers really respond to - just for example, Brook Park, Ohio Shop's owner Gerry Frank sent out 400 of the sales letters to his customers and sold 30 Club Cards at $79.95 each, in the first 3 days. Customers actually came by his shop after hours and shoved their enrollment forms and checks in under his door. To the average shop owner, this can provide upwards from an extra $60,000.00 in profits the first year, set up automatic renewal income, and build customer loyalty," Ron explains. "The only way this isn't a winner for the shop owner and his customers is if he doesn't do anything with it."

What Is The Biggest Income-Limiting Factor Holding Auto Repair Operators Back?

"Obviously there are lots of ways to try and measure or define 'success'," Ron says. "For many of these people, not working for somebody else, and getting to work around cars itself feels like success. But many of these business owners gradually realize they are working too hard to make their living and even after years of doing good work and building up a good reputation, they still go to bed worrying whether enough business'll come in to meet payroll or pay the bills during the month, and that is not 'success.' What causes that is the failure to be very actively interested in the marketing of the business, and the commitment to continuous marketing."

One of the very best marketing tools Ron has developed and provides for his shop owner-clients is a monthly consumer newsletter, customized for each shop owner, and sent to the shop owners' customers and near-by homeowners. The newsletter's content is a careful, strategic mix of advertising and promotion, the offer of the month, car care tips with lots of information and entertainment unrelated to the car. "There is not one shop owner who commits to sending this out every month who does not get a very, very good return on that investment," Ron says, "and we have plenty of proof from shop owners of that fact. Still, far too many refuse to invest less than 70 cents or so per customer per month, or have the discipline to stick with it. I believe this represents negative attitudes about marketing and the completely unjustified idea that just doing good, honest work ought to be enough to earn success in the marketplace. If I can help a shop owner re-think those things and become a marketer of his services, I can not only increase his income but otherwise improve his life, like by helping him make more but work less, so he has more time for his family - thanks to improved profit margins, the ability to charge premium prices, and the ability to attract quality oriented customers."

CONTACT INFORMATION:

Ron Ipach
CinRon Marketing Group
3041 Symmes Road, Suite C
Hamilton OH 45015
Phone: 513-860-1300
FAX: 513-860-3494
E-mail: info@ronipach.com
Website: www.ronipach.com

* * * * * *

Chapter #4

A Business Revolutionary
Creating Explosive Growth
In A 'Conservative' Industry

In 1990, Chauncey Hutter, Jr. worked in his father's two room, $50,000.00 a year tax preparation business. Today, Chauncey has turned the tiny 3-desk business into a chain of 18 offices, employing over 330 seasonal tax preparers and 25-or-so full-time managers, preparing over 29,000 tax returns, and generating millions of dollars of annual revenue. He has even driven the big, national brand-name chains out of some markets altogether, as they find themselves unable to compete with Chauncey's easily underestimated, powerful direct-response advertising and multi-media barrage, incorporating TV, radio, newspaper inserts, coupons, multi-step direct-mail and a "referral stimulation system" that multiplies customers like rabbits breeding.

Beginning in 1996, Chauncey started teaching his methods for creating explosive growth in this type of business to other independent tax preparers, accountants and C.P.A.'s. The network of these professionals now using his 'How To Take Your Tax Practice Past The Million Dollar Level' System numbers more than 1,400 nationwide. A current version of this system is available in home study course formats, ranging in price from under $1,000.00 to about $5,000.00.

In 2002, Chauncey launched a new, comprehensive coaching and business development program for this industry, in which a member will receive some degree of territorial exclusivity, use rights to all Chauncey's copyright protected and tested marketing tools, management and efficiency systems, and on-going coaching in every aspect of the business from Chauncey's entire executive team. Each coaching client will also get personal, hands-on assistance and consulting from Chauncey. This is only for the very serious businessperson seeking dramatic growth, as the program carries a price tag between $30,000.00 and $50,000.00. If you compare that price to a franchise, though, where there's not only a hefty fee but also a never-ending royalty on gross revenues, this is a bargain. The program is open to established tax preparation businesses as well as to new investors/operators who will open and own offices.

"This is a highly profitable business when done right," Chauncey explains. "Quite frankly, ours is a family business that allows me to take 4 months off every year, and still provides us with more money than we could ever spend. It is complicated, there's more to it than meets the eye, but we have proven 1-2-3, A-B-C systems for every part of the business, including those that can be real problems or holes in the profit bucket for other business owners. For example, there's advertising for new clients, but there's also advertising for, recruiting, training tax preparers, seasonal staffing, running a tax preparer school, customer retention year to year, stimulating referrals, and customer service issues, including ensuring accuracy and speed of service. "

One key to his success has been laser-beam clarity about the business he's really in, and the customer he targets with his advertising. "We are not in the tax preparation business. That's the service we provide but it is not what the customer wants. We sell instant cash. Our customer wants electronic filing and his tax refund immediately. We know who this customer is, the demographics, the media to reach him, the places he works, and the message to which he responds."

I'd make the point that this is a very important, often missed key to business success. Too many business owners focus on telling the marketplace about what they do, rather than on the end benefits the customer wants.

Another key has been what Chauncey calls 'the early Wal-Mart strategy.' He explains, " In our expansion, we avoided the big, major markets, and carefully selected cities where we could get the advertising opportunities we wanted at reasonable costs, and reach the right type of customers. We had a very specific site selection and target marketing strategy. We also chose to locate right next to the brand name competition and take them on. My style of marketing benefits from their presence. They create more customers for us than we do for them."

One of these giants was so frustrated with Chauncey's extraordinary marketing success, they tried to buy him.

What Has He Learned By Coaching Tax Business Owners?

"These are very technical minded people," Chauncey says, "with accounting backgrounds, training and conditioning. They can only take their businesses to a much higher level by making the mental shift from being the technician to being the marketer of the services."

"Dan has been to and spoken at my boot camps. He's seen this firsthand, how they struggle with this shift. They often retreat to the familiar and comfortable, the doing of the work. But that is, at best, a $15.00 an hour job. For the business owner to insist on doing much of the work himself, he's grossly underpaid, and he puts a very firm lid on his possible earnings. When he makes the shift, and becomes the marketer, he's now worth thousands of dollars an hour, and the sky's the limit on earnings. I'm overseeing a million in sales last week and we'll do another million this week. During peak season I've been taking my two little boys to McDonalds for breakfast and using their playland since its cold out. Then we goof off at home, put them down for naps and then my wife and I spend time together reading or walking. Even during peak tax season, I spend very little time in any of our offices or our main office. I definitely do not work like a dog, dawn to midnight, like a lot of these accountants do every tax season. I have people and systems in place, so I stay free to attend to the marketing, to maximizing sales, services rendered and profits."

Chauncey describes a transformational process: "First, I get my coaching client from technician to marketer, then to entrepreneur."

The proof his process works is, as they say, in the pudding. For example:

"We went from 150 to 776 clients in just one tax season following your system."

- James Erickson, Erickson Tax Service, Missouri

Or:

"Your unique referral system drove an extra $21,000.00 to my bottom line."

- Chris Joy, Fast Tax USA, Florida.

Or:

"Following your system, I opened two more locations, hired managers to run the offices and leave the office during peak tax season for lunch! (Something I could never do before!) And we increased revenues 20.91% in 1999, 38.11% in 2000, and 33.05% in 2001."

- Eric Elsea, Chattanooga, TN

New Technology Makes 'Tax Prep' A Convenience Store Commodity

A large percentage of tax returns are very simple to do. They are "W-2" based returns for working men and women, with tax refunds due them. A new breakthrough in technology allows these returns to be processed in virtually any retail business such customers frequent, as an added, seasonal profit center for the business, with no investment other than software. The customer information is entered following nearly brain-dead simple instructions, transmitted electronically to Chauncey's service center, processed overnight, and the customer's tax refund check is ready for him back at the store the next day.

"This puts finance companies, rent-to-own stores, discount furniture stores, insurance businesses, car dealerships, appliance stores, check cashing stores, in the instant tax refund business with no equipment, no floor space, and no designated personnel," explains Chauncey, "and for these businesses it serves three purposes: first, an added service to their customers; second, a way to attract traffic and new customers; and third, a natural way to promote, by cashing the tax refund checks and giving a bonus when the customer uses the money instantly for purchases in that store."

Chauncey's company has a complete, turn-key package for any such business, whether a big chain or a single mom-n-pop store, including software, the nominal training required, tech support by phone, advertising, in store display materials and direct-mail campaigns. "If they want to use this only with their own customers, they can use my proven marketing materials as statement stuffers, in store handouts or a postcard mailing. If they want to use it to attract new customers, we can even do a geographic/demographic direct-mail campaign for them, to drive traffic through their doors."

While Chauncey's company is not the only national service bureau providing comparable software and tax prep services, his is the only one providing turn-key, proven advertising and marketing. If you happen to own, or are the C.E.O. of a good-sized chain of stores, you'd be wise to consult with Chauncey personally about getting into this business and using it to maximum advantage. If you are a small business owner, you can obtain the entire system "in a box" and be in this business literally overnight.

"If a business has a computer, a telephone, a FAX machine and blue collar, working men and women as customers," Chauncey says, "we have everything else required to put a lot of added profits in their cash register, January through April."

It strikes me that this is a competitive advantage for the retail business now, but not offering this service and being able to do "get an instant tax refund here, spend it here and get a 10% bonus" promotions will be a competitive disadvantage in the very near future.

"We also help our coaching clients, who own a tax preparation business, with creating 'retail satellites' using our software and back office services, as joint ventures with retailers in their areas." Chauncey says. "This can add tens of thousands of dollars in bottom-line profits to their businesses with no added personnel."

Chauncey is introducing entirely new ways of doing business to the tax preparation industry coast-to-coast. Tax professionals eager to grow their current business, FAX your contact information to: 434-984-1590 for a FREE REPORT: "How To Take Your Tax Business To The Million Dollar Level!"

Entrepreneurs (NOT in the tax industry) seeking a turn-key, multi-location investment opportunity, send contact information by FAX to: 434-220-4706 for more details.....plus receive a FREE TAPE: "How A Kid With NO Tax Experience Grew a Father's Small Tax Business To The Million Dollar Level Leaving All The 'Tax Experts' In The Dust!"

Existing Business Owner (or C.E.O.) with retail location(s) serving lower income blue collar customers; looking for a sales surge and additional profit center in the first quarter of each year: E-mail a profile on your business organization to: iplus@protax.com or FAX 434-220-4706 and a priority package detailing the "All Cash Profit Center" Opportunity will follow.

If you prefer asking for any of the above information by mail, send requests.

CONTACT INFORMATION:

Chauncey Hutter, Jr.
PRO-TAX Plus, Inc.
251 Ridge McIntire Rd
Charlottesville VA 22903
Phone: 434-220-4705
FAX: 434-220-4706
e-mail: iplus@protax.com

* * * * * *

Chapter #5

Escape From Managed Care

Dr. Barry Lycka is an eminently well qualified physician, with a successful private practice, significant community involvement and prominence, and a safe, secure, certain financial position.

Dr. Barry Lycka did the most amazing thing.

He turned his entire professional life upside down.

As you probably know, managed care — the combine of insurance companies, HMO's and PPO's — have wrestled control of the health care system away from the physicians, so today's doctor suffers under severe limitations and interference in his practice, price controls that cap his fees, and a blizzard of paperwork. Most doctors resent all this, but it's like the weather; easy to complain about, hard to do anything about. While opting out of managed care may be every M.D.'s private fantasy, few have the courage or the know-how to do anything more than daydream.

In Canada, government and managed care controls are even more onerous than in the United States. Dr. Lycka, who practices in Edmonton, Alberta, Canada told me that not only are the fees for different services regulated, but the total dollar amount of health care services that can be delivered and billed in each geographic area are capped, and if those doctors combined services exceed that amount, they are all penalized!

So Dr. Lycka opted out.

Actually, a bit more than 70% of his total, thriving practice is outside the Canadian government managed care, insurance and reimbursement system; in simple terms, a fee for service, cash practice. As he puts it, "If I can successfully escape in Canada, my strategies work even better for doctors in the United States."

One of the secrets is starting, having or expanding a cosmetic surgery practice. The demand for cosmetic surgery is booming, as the biggest population of "baby boomers" hit their mid-life years and peak discretionary incomes - and are very unwilling to age quietly and gracefully! Stigmas are gone, fears diminished, public acceptance at an all-time high. Hollywood celebrities once hid and denied their cosmetic surgeries; now they openly acknowledge them, even brag about them. For a long list of reasons, continued growth in cosmetic surgery profession revenues are certain. And opportunities in cosmetic surgery exist for surgeons, other M.D.'s, even dermatologists, gynecologists and family doctors.

Because cosmetic surgery is elective, it is fee for service, and the ideal basis for a cash practice, free of interference from managed care.

In 1991, Dr. Lycka made the strategic decision to navigate his practice through a transition from family medicine to specializing in cosmetic surgery. Over 4 years, he struggled to find his way, to develop practice marketing strategies that worked, to develop case presentations that led to acceptance, and on and on. By 1995, he had invested hundreds of thousands of dollars in trial-and-error as well as consulting from leading marketing advisors, ultimately arriving at an a-to-z system for marketing and managing a premium quality, high profit practice.

"I knew that this would be a very difficult and challenging transition, especially given the exceptionally stringent limitations in Canada, and the limited size of my market, but I was determined to put myself in a position of independence and autonomy," Dr. Lycka told me. "There was no marked path to follow. No how-to manual. No instruction book."

His own practice exceeded $1.6 million that year, and Dr. Lycka sticks rigidly to a 40-hour work week, and practices free of bureaucratic interference. Word spread about Dr. Lycka's successful "jail break", and he received numerous invitations to speak at physicians' conferences, and authored two professional manuals, "Shaping A New Image: the Practice Of Cosmetic Surgery" and "The Million Dollar Practice Notebook", both recipient of critical acclaim from medical society presidents, university professors and other leaders from the medical community. The books and lectures only led to increased demand from doctors for more extensive help from Dr. Lycka with their practices.

Dr. Lycka's Daring Trail-Blazing Makes Liberation Easier, Faster And Certain For Other Doctors Throughout North America

This is a complex subject. A review of Dr. Lycka's published papers, lectures, books and seminar and coaching notes reveals a remarkable diversity of knowledge required to establish a successful cosmetic surgery practice. There are medical, technical, advertising, marketing, management and financial issues. For example, the topics list from his published paper and lectures includes: doing an effective skin biopsy; painless anesthesia; increasing patient safety and satisfaction with liposuction; Mohs' micrographic surgery; selection of laser equipment; combining laser surgery with other aspects of a surgical dermatology practice; and the list continues.

Since I'm an advertising man, I asked about the advertising and marketing aspects. "A lot of doctors are needlessly participating in an ever-escalating advertising war in their markets, buying bigger and bigger newspaper and Yellow

Pages ads, spending more and more. I have perfected more efficient, lower cost advertising and other means of attracting ample quantities of good, qualified new patients," Dr. Lycka answered. "Other doctors are very uninformed about advertising and marketing and can easily be victimized, wasting small fortunes on super-fancy, slick brochures, videos and web sites that look great but don't work. Finally there are doctors who are marketing adverse, and need to re-think their entire philosophy. In coaching doctors on practice transitions, I've dealt with all three of these scenarios and achieved highly successful results."

In response to demand, Dr. Lycka has built a complete "paint-by-the-numbers" system useful for the veteran cosmetic surgeon seeking to expand and improve the profitability of a practice, or for the doctor ready to gradually or quickly transition out from under the oppressive thumb of managed care. "This is a proven path a doctor can now move along at his own pace," Dr. Lycka explains, "that virtually eliminates trial-and-error, saves considerable sums by preventing all manner of mis-steps from purchasing the wrong equipment to using overly expensive advertising, and, frankly, requires less courage."

The Rolls-Royce Of Professional Coaching Programs

Dr Lycka's system can be acquired and implemented on several levels. "I have the entire system in a box, essentially a combination of a home study course and a practical tool kit, including books, audio cassettes, and so forth, and that is a good starting point for the doctor yet uncertain of what he wants to do. At the next level, that set of materials is supported by telecoaching, and I do some of that personally, some via small group tele-conferences, and some is provided by an associate of mine, an expert in marketing, who is thoroughly versed in my methods. Finally, at the highest level, this is all preceeded and supplemented by either an on-site, private one to three day consultation at the individual doctor's office or the individual doctor's visit to my practice, as a field trip, and private consultation with me. When my associate goes to the doctor's site, he conducts a thorough practice analysis, actually customizes my materials for the doctor and rewrites or writes advertising and marketing materials for the doctor, and establishes a schedule of implementation, with follow-up and accountability."

These private, customized consultations are, as you might immediately assume, pricey. Dr. Lycka and his associates can only accommodate two or, at most, three such clients per month, and at times, there is a waiting list. Fees range from $10,000.00 to $30,000.00 for this service - however, the results can be quite dramatic.

For example:

"I can never thank Dr. Barry Lycka enough. He has been a coach, a mentor, a friend. His books "Shaping A New Image" and "More Shaping" are my bibles. He has increased my cosmetic surgery income 337%.

- Peter Ursel, M.D., Lindsey, Ontario, Canada

Or:

"I could go on and on about the other things I learned from Dr. Barry Lycka. He showed me how to bundle cosmetic procedures for maximum patient results and revenue. He worked with my patient coordinator in a consultation....He showed me how to present things for maximum effectiveness. Made the business and presenting cosmetic surgery fun again. And in the first 10 days after his consultation I brought in an additional $28,000.00 in procedures."

- Dr. Michael Walker, Fredericksburg, Texas

And, after all, as few as three cosmetic patients a doctor wouldn't attract otherwise repays this entire investment. The lesser levels of the system are obtainable for as little as $1,577.00.

Every one of these services is provided on a fully guaranteed basis. "There will never be a professional colleague dissatisfied or disappointed in any way with the assistance we provide," Dr. Lycka flatly states. "I will not permit it."

The Triangle Of Professional Success

"My liberation of my practice, its exceptional financial rewards, impossible if 100% managed care controlled, is what gives me the freedom to maintain what I call the 'triangle of professional success'", Dr. Lycka says.

That triangle is excellence in patient services; generosity in community service; service to the profession.

Dr. Lycka's practice is a shining example of excellence. A "field trip" to the practice in person or via video tape reveals a unique, first class environment, a highly motivated, knowledgeable and capable staff, and smoothly running, efficient services. "It is most satisfying", Dr. Lycka says, "to practice in an office, in an environment that you are proud of, with patients who specifically seek you out and who are respectful of your time and expertise. Every doctor deserves this kind of career experience. While others express their mounting frustration with the daily routine of practice, I honestly enjoy it every single day."

In community service, Dr. Lycka is creative and generous. Since 1996, he has provided tattoo removal without charge for women in the process of rehabilitation from prostitution. Since 1997, he has been providing free reconstructive and laser procedures for women who have been victims of spousal abuse, for which he has received national and international acclaim. In 2001, the Second Annual Barry Lycka Golf Tournament For Cancer Research had 142 participating golfers, and raised over $68,000.00.

In service to his profession, Dr. Lycka continues to free up time from his schedule to accept lecture engagements on clinical or business topics, at medical conferences and association meetings.

It seems obvious to me that this "Triangle Of Success" has application to all of us, regardless of the nature of our businesses.

CONTACT INFORMATION:

Dr. Barry Lycka
780 – 10665 Jasper Avenue
Edmonton, AB T5J 3S9
CANADA

Phone: 780-425-1212
FAX: 780-425-1217
E-mail: basl@v-wave.com
Website: www.cosmeticsx.com

* * * * * *

Chapter #6

Cash Flow King

In business, there's a saying: cash flow is king. If there is a king of cash flow, it is Ron LeGrand. If you have only a passing knowledge of real estate investing, your picture will feature the landlord, dealing with busted toilets and tenants who sneak out in the dead of night. But Ron's approach, which has made him wealthy, and which he has taught to well over 500,000 people, is very, very different. His term for what he does is "Quick-Turn Real Estate", sometimes called "flipping." He holds nor needs real estate licenses, attended no school, yet, while a typical real estate agent may work hard all year to earn $50,000.00, Ron makes that on one or two "flips" in a matter of weeks.

I have known Ron for over ten years, been a guest speaker at his annual conventions of his 'students', and gotten to know a number of the people he has pointed to the financial promised land, and I am unceasingly amazed at the moneymaking power of his methods and the incredible successes of his students.

A Frustrated Car
Mechanic Answers
A Newspaper Ad

Twenty years ago or so, Ron LeGrand was working for wages as a "grease monkey", living paycheck to paycheck, struggling to get on his feet financially, and unable to even imagine the kind of wealth and success he enjoys today.

He saw an ad in the newspaper about a seminar where you could learn to get rich by investing in real estate, even if you had no money and no credit. The incongruity of needing to come up with $450.00 to attend the seminar itself did not occur to him. He borrowed the $450.00, some from friends, some from family.

Have you ever seen one of those ads and wondered if the promises are real or hype? Today, you see TV infomercials holding out the same kind of promises. In fact, Ron himself is the subject of one of those infomercials! And, as he will tell you, all such ads or shows about getting rich in real estate even if you have no money, no credit and no experience, contain some hype, some truth, and much depends on the individual. In Ron's case, he hungrily digested what was taught at this seminar and then he did a most unusual thing; he actually went to work, hard, following the moneymaking plan provided at the seminar. "By my standards today, what I learned there was crude and primitive," Ron says. "For example, calling up homeowners cold on the phone and making so-called 'nothing down' offers is filled with rejection, takes a lot of time, and a whole lot more persistence than most people have. Today we know how to, instead, get motivated sellers calling us. Still, I did the most important thing. I took action. And I stuck with it."

Within a few months, Ron had acquired 70 properties! Not long after that, he was up to 276 rental units. But this meteoric success was actually a cash flow nightmare. "I had become a paper millionaire in under a year," Ron recalls, "but you can't eat equity or pay bills with it. I was broke. That led me to re-evaluating everything I was doing and looking for cash flow, for a way to make a good living doing this day to day."

A determined Ron LeGrand pioneered new ground, ultimately arriving at a formula or a process that provides current cash flow from flipping properties, with the choice always there to keep one as a long-term investment. In the ensuing 19 years, Ron personally bought and sold over 1,400 houses. And he perfected a system for making a very high income from even a few transactions a year, and for taking fast cash profits from every deal. "It absolutely does not matter where you live, whether you're wealthy or broke, college educated or uneducated, whether the economy is good or bad," Ron says.

Breaking Rules And Exploding Myths About Making Money In Real Estate

Most people think the only way to make money in real estate is to tie up all your money in properties, or even to go into debt to buy properties, sit on them for ten or twenty years, contend with bad tenants, plugged-up toilets and negative cash flow, then finally, ultimately sell for a profit. And virtually all the heavily advertised and promoted courses about making money in real estate teach by these same basic rules: buy low, hold, sell higher, later. Ron LeGrand's approach is completely contrary to this traditional wisdom, featuring strategies for cash profits from each deal in a matter of days, weeks or, at most, months, not years.

The results achieved by his students are nothing short of amazing.....

Real People, Real Money

Over 7,000 "Quick-Turn Real Estate Entrepreneurs" have traveled to Orlando, for Ron's 4-day annual convention. I am there, as a guest speaker, and an observer. And I have poured over hundreds and hundreds of letters to Ron from his students. These are the kind of stories I hear or read, one after another after another....

Dennis and Monica Quattlebaum from Georgia talk about how Ron's training has changed their lives completely. They cite incredibly profitable deals, beginning with their very first one, which they paid $112,000.00 for, and sold for $162,000.00, cash. Another with a $60,000.00 profit. In just their first year, they've bought and sold twenty houses! But, interestingly, they also talk about the non-monetary aspects of the business. "We are able to help a lot of people get their houses off their backs, and provide houses for others." Dennis says. "I even had a grown man cry at his kitchen table when we were able to take his house problem away to protect his credit, while he was unable to meet his payments due to an illness."

A 26-year old Michigan resident, Pablo Carbajal, took control of a property for just $20.00, sold it wholesale to another investor in 45 days, and made a $5,346.20 cash proft. Pablo told Ron, "I studied your material until my eyes turned red and listened to the CD's until my ears bled!"

Arthur Kisser: "In the past 15 months since I have been exposed to your courses and attended your boot camps, my income is 7-times the salary I received as an executive in a Fortune 500 company, and my lifestyle has improved dramatically."

Chuck Smith, a Cleveland, Ohio police officer who, in 8 months, part-time, made almost $150,000.00.

A 20 year old college student, Layne Parker, in Juneau, Alaska, who made $85,000.00 on her very first "quick turn" transaction.

Literally, Actually Creating Millionaires
Coast To Coast

I've racked my brain and I can't think of any other successful entrepreneur turned coach who can match Ron's record of quite literally creating "from scratch" millionaires. These days, nearly 5,000 new people discover Ron each month, thanks to his TV program, web site, referrals from his students, and books. Over 50,000 have attended his boot camps in recent years. Ron and I did the calculations as I was working on this chapter for this book, and conservatvely estimate that his students, all combined, have purchased well over one billion — with a 'b'! — dollars of real estate! And you will find it a difficult challenge to go into any city anywhere in North America and fail to find at least several real estate entrepreneurs advertising "we buy houses for cash", who are Ron LeGrand students.

Yet there is no shortage of opportunity. "Using my methods, some people buy and flip luxury homes, some do fixer-uppers, some buy to hold for investment, some flip as quickly as possible, and in most areas, we could multiply the number of Ron LeGrand trained entrepreneurs by 100 and still not put a dent in the market," Ron says. "You have to keep in mind that the average cash profit per transaction is between $20,000.00 and $30,000.00, so ten, twenty or thirty a year is about all any one person needs or wants to do. In this business, they can make a giant income but still take lots of time off, and most do." Ron adds, "This is a business you can enter instantly, learn quickly, and create income quickly, even if handicapped by lack of cash or credit."

My own perspective is that it is one of the few "pure" marketing businesses legitimately offering high income potential. By "pure", I mean your finanncial resources, time and energy are freed up purely for the direct application to attracting motivated sellers and doing deals; there's no store or office to worry about, no employees to parent, no inventory to handle or ship, no products to manufacture, no catalogs or sales literature to continually create or update and produce, and so on. Frankly, were I personally choosing a new field of endeavor today, I would find this business very appealing.

Another Business Birthed
By Ron's Success

Ron LeGrand is a restless man endlessly fascinated with building businesses and teaching success strategies to others. His "little seminar business" has become a publishing, seminar and coaching juggernaut, with a host of new products including books, audio cassettes, home study courses, software programs and boot camps on all different aspects of real estate investing, a newsletter with thousands of subscribers - in total, an "information business" exceeding 20-million dollars in annual revenue.

It was a natural, maybe inevitable next step for Ron to begin showing others how to convert their own expertise, know-how and experience into information products, to develop information product mail-order businesses just like his. A second company, Global Publishing, run by Ron's daughter, Vicki, conducts boot camps and offers training in this area of entrepreneurial activity. People have already traveled from as far away as Australia to attend these seminars, as the word has spread, that Ron is willng to reveal the marketing strategies behind his information empire.

"The Less I Do,
The More I Make"

Ron's personal credo: the less I do, the more I make.

As you can tell, Ron is not a lazy man, so what does this mean? In short, from my vantage point, it highlights Ron's commitment to having concise, streamlined, effective marketing tools, to do the work ---- in place of manual labor.

He teaches "quick turn real estate entrepreneurs" this principle, and gives them the means to apply it. For example, no one following Ron's model would ever "cold call' people advertising homes for sale in the newspaper; they set up marketing that brings the deals to them.

CONTACT INFORMATION:

For free information about all of Ron's training programs and boot camps about Quick-Turn Real Estate, go to www.SDIWealthInstitute.com or call 800-387-4306.

For more information from Global Publishing, about starting your own information marketing or internet marketing business from your home, go to their website: www.globalpublishinginc.com or call 888-840-8389.

* * * * * *

Chapter #7

Coach To Wall Street And
The Fortune 500

It is 6:00 A.M., and dawn is barely breaking, wealthy Marin County, Caliornia is still asleep, except for a few newspaper delivery boys, police officers on patrol, and a thin, wiry fellow bicyclng along a bumpy backroad near Highway 1. The skinny, bespectacled Clark Kent-ish cyclist is a CPA, legal expert, former Standford professor, super-entrepreneur and consultant, feverishly juggling a 50 to 60 hour workweek with up to 20 hours of training each week as a competitive cyclist. Back in 1989, he bought a regional cyclist magazine - which he promptly expanded into a multi-state, multi-publication media company. In 1990, he was named to the U.S. Masters Team of cyclists, invited to compete in the Soviet Union National Masters Championship.

I first met Stephen Roulac two years ago, and have since enjoyed having him as one of the members of my elite Platinum Inner Circle, limited to 15 Members. I and the other Members have been blown away by his incisive thinking, his breadth of knowledge and his speed-of-light ability to zero in on the core question leading to a solution or opportunity. If you aspire to substantial financial success, you should meet Stephen Roulac.....

As Ron LeGrand is "everyman's" real estate riches coach, Stephen Roulac is corporate America's leading advisor in this same arena. His experience and influence span three decades, working with major institutional investors, real estate syndicates, investment banks and commercial property owners. For example, in 1974, his near-psychic forecasting of explosive late 70's growth in certain kinds of real estate values produced a 2-billion dollar windfall for his client, the Reichman Brothers. In the mid-1980's, his insights into the precarious status of the office sector - identified at least five years before others recognized the situation - saved his institutional clients billions of dollars. Even more recently, strategies Stephen devised for Merrill Lynch investors created over 1-billion dollars in above market norms investment returns.

The media has frequently recognized his extraordinary acumen and value. *San Francisco Business* ranked him as "one of the best-known and widely consulted real estate experts in the country.....few other experts come close to matching his expertise or his breadth and depth of knowledge in commercial or residential real estate." *Kiplinger's Personal Finance Magazine* described him as "perhaps the most influential of the country's independent real estate analysts."

What Makes Roulac So Unique That
America's Biggest Investors
Seek His Counsel - And What Might You
Learn From His Approach
To Enhance Your Own Success?

"There is micro perspective and macro perspective, and too many investors or entrepreneurs choose only one or the other," Stephen says. "In my case, while I employ a top down emphasis on macro issues, the mathematical models, the manipulation of financial formulas and statistics, in negotiations of million and multi-million dollar transactions, I still also believe in the importance of the micro, the hands-on attention to the practical, pragmatic details of success with retail or commercial real estate."

While Stephen has an excellent academic background, featuring a PhD. from Stanford, a JD from University of California, Berkley and a MBA from Harvard, he began his career in the nitty-gritty of construction: labor crew supervision, site management, apartment and commercial property management. He even insists that his passionate love of the outdoors and time spent hiking, running and cycling contributes to his creative thinking, applied to improving the value of physical environments.

"If you apply all this to any business, the idea is not to get isolated in the distant ivory tower analyzing only the statistics of your business, in an academic, theoretical or too broad of a manner, but instead to stay continuously connected to the front lines, to the delivery of your service, to the relationships with the customers," Stephen explains. "But on the other hand, not to get so mired in the day to day detail that you sacrifice vision and fail to identify evolving opportunity or risk. This is a blending of theory and practical, of big picture and minute detail, of history, present, near future and long-term forecasting. This is the challenge of leadership, whether a person is running his own small business or the CEO of a large entity."

In total, Stephen Roulac has been involved in over 2,000 consulting assignments, involving real estate interests exceeding 50-billion dollars in value, working with senior management in companies like Apple Computer, Bank of America, Texaco, Hallmark Corporation, as well as many municipal governments, the Government of Singapore Investment Corporation, and large institutional and private investors. In a sector of the economy where many brokers, pundits and government agencies offer information and advice for free - thereby training people not to expect to pay for expertise - he has been paid over 100-million dollars for his advice.

One obvious question about all that is how he can so effectively move from one very different project to another, from retail to office to even residential real estate situations, from one geographial area to the next. The answer has important implications for every businessperson. "Decision-making procedures, models and systems have been a primary emphasis of my work," Stephen explains, "so that we now have well thought out, tested, proven mechanical processes we use to make each new decision. A simplistic comparison might be a pilot's safety checklist which he uses each and every time prior to take-off, regardless of location or destination, weather conditions or other variables. Few businesspeople have set, reliable processes for arriving at good decisions."

Coaching Others With
Proprietary Research And
Decision-Making Guidance

Today, Stephen Roulac and his team of experts consult and coach on a number of different levels.

ROULAC GROUP also publishes an entire array of educational materials, ranging in price from $19.00 to $997.00. THE ROULAC INVESTOR PROFILE is an inter-active questionnaire or "test", that enables you to analyze how well you are doing in strategizing and managing your investments. This Profile is the first part of an entire, unique "investment check-up in a box." Information about these products is at www.roulac.com.

There is also an audio subscription available, providing 52 weeks of the 60-minute talk show, Location Matters: The Stephen Roulac Conversation, broadcast on NPR, National Public Radio. The show is about the future of how we live and work, the renaissance of cities, and what this means to investors and entrepreneurs. The subscription, show highlights and other information is at www.locationmatters.com.

His firm also offers ROULAC PLACE/PROPERTY/STRATEGY, a subscription based advisory service that makes Stephen's on-going strategy advice affordable for individual investors. This service is available at www.roulacplacepropertystrategy.com.

On another level, Stephen continues, his demanding schedule permitting, to privately advise corporate, bank and government clients, and to accept speaking engagements from national associations and investment, financial or banking corporations and organizations. He has addressed over 500 audiences throughout the U.S., Asia, Europe, Australia and Latin America.

At a formal dinner following a talk in Belfast, Ireland, a member of the House Of Lords of the British Parliament said, "Professor Roulac gave one of the best lectures I've ever heard.....a remarkably learned and entertaining blend of the history of science, sociology and economic themes. He artfully wove together disparate themes into a cohesive message about property, society and its institutions."

A new direction for Stephen and his firm is providing global investment management services to a select "by invitation only" group of substantial individual and institutional investors.

Whether coaching an individual private client, such as a Fortune 500 CEO, conducting group tele-coaching sessions, or teaching via his writings and cassettes, Stephen says his primary focus is facilitating what he describes as more effective and responsible decision-making. "Every dollar of diminished or enhanced investment value in my world, as well as every measure of failure or success, peace of mind or anxiety, frustration or happiness is the result of decision-making. It is the most important human skill, yet it is rarely, formally taught as a skill. It is the most important responsibility of the CEO, entrepreneur or parent, yet few have formalized, disciplined procedures for it."

Quality Of Thought Requires
Quality "Raw Material"

It has been said, with slight nuance differences, by a long list of "philosophers", from mail-order entrepreneur Joe Karbo to IBM founder Thomas Watson to Stephen Roulac that too many people are too busy to think. According to Stephen, the kind of quality thinking that leads to good decision-making requires broad, diversified stimulus and perspective, accurate data and analytical information, a structured and disciplined approach, and time.

One of the ways he personally acquires diverse input is through incredibly extensive travel. Stephen has traveled, worked, consulted and assisted with investment in a laundry list of destinations that would make a Conde Nast editor green with envy, including, neatly in alpha order: Australia, Austria, Belarus, Canada, China, England, France, Finland, Germany, Hong Kong, Hungary, Indonesia, Ireland, Italy, Japan, Morocco, Nepal, Norway, Russia, Spain, Sweden, Switzerland, and on and on. "Consider the opportunity or stimulus for breakthrough insights and ideas many businesspeople never encounter by severely limiting the scope of their observation, whether physically, or intellectually," Stephen says.

"After all, Starbucks exists because its founder was impressed by the unique culture and ambiance and societal importance of the coffee bar he observed in Italy. Disney's interesting community development project, Celebration, is European village inspired, in its mixed use residential-retail aspects. Whether a businessperson expands his intelligence gathering and inspiration through travel and personal observation as I do or by doing something as simple as Dan Kennedy's habit of buying 20 or 30 magazines he never regularly reads from a newsstand to go through on a long flight or driving to and from office and home via different routes, his challenge is to invest the time to improve his input."

Stephen reaches all the way back to the classic success book written by Andrew Carnegie's hand-picked writer, Napoleon Hill, *Think And Grow Rich.* "Hill identified thirteen characteristics held in common by the most successful industrialists, inventors and entrepreneurs of the 1900's, and one of the thirteen he labeled as 'accurate thinking.' Accurate thinking requires accurate, valid, well researched analytical information." Stephen says, "It is unceasingly surprising to me how many people make substantial financial decisions without first gathering or obtaining and evaluating relevant historical references, current information and expert forecasts."

**Stephen Roulac
In The Courtroom**

One other aspect of Stephen's business activities and expertise of interest, even viewed by some as glamorous, is his frequent appearance in the courtroom as an expert witness.

We have always romanticized the courtroom battlefield, in hundreds of movies, popular novels, and with some of TV's most enduring, popular characters, from Perry Mason to Matlock to the lawyers of *The Practice.* Business cases, of course, rarely feature the dramatic breakdown of a witness on the stand ala Perry Mason. Instead, business litigation wins and losses often revolve around the ability of a highly credible, authoritative expert witness to decipher complex, specialized financial transactions and explain them in a manner that is understandable and persuasive to judge and jury. This is where Stephen Roulac steps in.

Fortunately for his clients, his resume and expert credentials in real estate are unimpeachable. His confident demeanor unshakeable. And his ability to communicate extraordinary. As are his results. For example, his preparation and testimony helped Joan Irvine Smith to realize a gigantic 250-million dollar settlement in litigation involving The Irvine Company — more than twice what had been proposed by Donald Bren, the principal defendant. Stephen is sought after for help with high-stakes litigation and high profile cases involving real estate, lending and related matters at least several times a month, turns down many more clients than he accepts, and chooses only those that intrigue him.

When asked if there was a lesson in his top status, and huge fees, as an expert witness for all entrepreneurs, Stephen said "If translated to coaching advice to any individual, I would say that the lesson is: be very proactive, aggressive, creative and determined in making yourself the pre-eminent expert in some specialized aspect of your industry, as well as gaining widespread recognition of that fact. If translated to financial, management or decision-making advice for a business leader, it would be to wisely but willingly invest in expensive expertise.

Stephen Roulac is one of, if not the most expensive expert witness there is. However, in the high stakes litigations where he has testified or assisted, the contributions have, almost without exception, produced victories and huge returns on the investment in his firm and his work.

CONTACT INFORMATION:

You can obtain more information about Stephen's numerous books, audio cassettes and other materials at his website: www.propertypress.com or by FAXing a request for a catalog to 415-451-4343. You can obtain information about ROULAC PLACE PROPERTY STRATEGY at www.roulacplacepropertystrategy.com or 415-451-4300.

If you are facing an important real estate decision or strategy issue for your company, want Stephen to serve as an expert witness in high stakes litigation, or are intersted in having Stephen speak for your organization, you can call his office directly at 415-451-4300, FAX him at the 415-451-4343, e-mail expert@roulac.com, or visit www.roulac.com.

* * * * * *

Chapter #8

The Man Who Knew What He Didn't Want

Imagine a person who, as consultant and coach, helps business owners re-engineer their businesses, to make more money while liberating themselves from doing things they don't want to do. What kind of a business is that? A good one.

Jeff Paul's personal life transformation, and zig-zag path to his current lifestyle, began with rock-solid realizations of what he did NOT want to do with the rest of his life. At age 32, Jeff was a partner in a successful planning practice, adept at the "rainmaker role"; bringing in new clients. But there was much he did not like. The commute. The, to him, boring nature of the work. The hassles with partners. Even the wearing of a tie. So he did an extraordinary thing: he made a list of things he did not want to do, and went in search of a new means of earning a living that would never require him to do those things again. His list became the lighthouse beacon he navigated toward. It is a strategy he suggests to other business owners today.

Jeff's list led him to the fields of direct marketing and information publishing, and he began with the idea of marketing a manual about his successful method for acquiring financial planning clients to other financial planners. He quit his other business, burned his bridges, and leapt into the new venture, only to quickly hit a brick wall. Sales far less than expected, returns for refunds huge. Before long, he was out of money; he, Peggy and the kids took up residence in his sister-in-law's basement, credit card debt climbed to over $100,000.00. But eventually he got it right. I take some credit, for a few suggestions made to Jeff when he attended one of my seminars.

With a few changes to his approach, Jeff turned this struggling attempt at mail-order into an "overnight success." In September, 1991, its sales were a meager $2,000.00 The very next month, sales leapt to $13,000.00. Then, in short order, $26,000.00, in November, $49,000.00 in December, and in the first 12 successful months, over $1,000,000.00. Debts were cleared, a new home purchased, a real business underway. Over the next 6 years, this business grew to include 20 different products, courses, seminars and services for financial planners, insurance agents and other financial professionals, and Jeff became one of the most prominent "coaches" to this industry.

This business blazed plenty of new trails in the financial services industry. The first to run sensationalized, emotional, tabloid-y advertorials in the professional journals. The longest sales letter ever mailed in the industry – 56 pages! The first training program with a $500.00 to $1,000.00 price tag, with no live classes included. It all led to an amazing 8,500+ "members" buying and using its products.

A Reliable Business Model Emerges

From this business, Jeff built a formula, a system for building a profitable information business in a niche market, which proved repeatable. He applied it again, and created an equally large information business serving the real estate industry (which he subsequently sold). The second time there was no trial-and-error; the business model worked perfectly. I recognized the value of his now proven business model and his story, and suggested he package that, and teach it to others involved in similar businesses or interested in starting one. This led to a now famous full-page magazine ad headlined "How To Make $4,000.00 A Day Sitting At Home, At Your Kitchen Table, In Your Underwear", which appeared repeatedly in dozens of national magazines, sold over 100,000 copies of Jeff's book by the same title, and sold thousands of his mail-order courses. Jeff and I conducted a number of seminars teaching his system, which spawned hundreds of successful mail-order entrepreneurs. For example, there's a former pro baseball player, now successfully marketing how-to videos and audios, books, "camps" and coaching to parents of Little League, high school and college baseball players; a Harley-Davidson mechanic who sells a "How To Fix Your Harley Yourself – So You Don't Get Ripped Off By Harley Dealers" set of videos; and a guy who sells a "No Money Down Real Estate Course" strictly on the internet - all thanks to "the Jeff Paul business model." (Which shows that Jeff's model works the same on-line as it does off-line!)

By necessity, Jeff also became a highly skilled direct-response copywriter. One sales letter of Jeff's has sold over $7-million of golf clubs (with no pictures of the clubs, no famous golfer's endorsement). For those of you who play golf, the putter sold for a mind-boggling $400.00, the irons about $375.00 each, the woods, $625.00 each. Testament to the power of great sales copy.

Creating Strategic Alliances

Today, Jeff's business interests are diverse - but all share two common threads. One is honoring his "What I Do NOT Want To Do List." No commute. No employees. No fixed hours. Two, utilizing the marketing skills he honed in his own businesses.

He is an author and publisher of a number of business courses and how-to manuals, including "Instant Profits Marketing", direct marketing strategies for any type of business; "How To Write Copy So Good You Can Sell Sand In The Desert"; and "The Joint Venture Marketing System", including all the agreements and forms needed to organize joint ventures. He has two membership websites: www.instantprofits.com, and www.killercopywriting.com.

He is also a partner with me in the Psycho-Cybernetics Foundation, and author of "A Course In Accurate Thinking", which can be found at the www.psycho-cybernetics.com web site.

His primary business of the moment is as a joint venture marketing consultant and, at times, joint venture participant, helping one company promote its products or services with little or no out-of-pocket expense through joint ventures with others, and obtaining saleable products and services, and proven promotions for "back end marketing" to its customers for added profits, with no product development or acquisition investment. In some cases, he is a provider of products and promotions, in others a finder and alliance broker. It is an odd way to make a living, odd enough that it is difficult to accurately describe. Yet it produces a high six figure, part-time income for Jeff, and millions of dollars of revenue for his clients. If you have a good customer list and need added profits, or you have good products and need more distribution, Jeff can help.

Jeff points out that "joint venture capital is often better than cash venture capital. Joint ventures benefit both parties with a degree of certainty not found in any other type of advertising, marketing or promotion."

He also functions as a private coach to direct marketers using "the Jeff Paul model" in building niche-market information businesses. One such client, for example, has a multi-million dollar a year business providing books, tapes, courses, newsletters, marketing kits, seminars and coaching to the chiropractic profession. Another, sells a training course to insurance agents showing them how to sell life insurance over the phone without making cold calls.

For example:

"Getting involved with your course was the single best investment I've ever made. To this day (over two years later), I still use your course darn near every week. The results of studying your material? **I gross between $30,000.00 to $60,000.00 a month** with my information product. My previous career had some things that were wonderful and great about it but quite honestly it's like night and day compared to what I'm doing now – I'm doing what I want to do, how I want to do it, and I really am my own boss. My time really belongs to me. I'm really having a ball, it's a lot of fun! I feel a deep sense of gratitude to you. Thank you so very much for your help!"

- Mike C., Decatur, Georgia

"I wanted to let you know how your system is working for me. So far, I've received 78 orders at $849.00 and I haven't even sent out the second notice! Even though I have a practicing career, as a result of direct response marketing, I have hired another person to treat my patients in the morning so I can run my business out of my home on the hill; and yes, sometimes in my underwear! I'm really enjoying it. Now, I work 3 afternoons at my office collecting $35,000.00 a month there, and thanks to you, **I'm on course to collect $50,000.00 - $60,000.00 a month in about 2 –3 months with my home business.** Even though I'm far from an expert in lead generation, there can't be anything out there that a "beginner" can do with such dramatic results in such a short period of time. I really do owe it to you."

- Dr. Ben A., Haywood, California

"I think the course is phenomenal! In early January '97 we started marketing the sales letter and by February 25th **we've had $6,000.00 in orders.** I wish I had started sooner. This course worked better than I expected."

- Paul C., Superior, Colorado

His focus is on helping business owners get what they really want from their businesses.

"It's sometimes still amazing to me," Jeff says, "that I have been able to orchestrate my entire business to totally serve me, support my lifestyle preferences, and let me control my schedule. I prize the freedom. Like last week, I took off to go to our vacation home in Wisconsin for a week. Put a message on my answering machine that I wasn't available. Most business owners wouldn't dare. Most need help making the decisions that can lead to this kind of freedom."

"I usually start with the marketing itself," Jeff continues, "because most businesses' marketing is unnecessarily manual labor intensive, or requires too many people, or too much work. Usually this can be automated with better ads, prospect qualifying, sales letters and technology. That starts to liberate a business owner. By dramatically increasing the value of each customer, a business winds up needing fewer customers and less infrastructure. Ultimately we deal with other aspects of the business too. The whole idea is to re-make the business from master to servant."

Another powerful secret that Jeff teaches may be the most potent weapon a business owner can use to make huge piles of money, the "Market First – Product Second" formula. Most businesses get or create a product or service; and then try to find people to sell it to. This formula, according to Jeff, is a precursor to eventual failure. Jeff's formula is: 1) Identify a strong, potential market. A group of people with irrational passions, money, repeated spending behaviors and who are reachable. 2) Find out what they already want, what they already are interested in. 3) Give them #2 over and over! Jeff asks a good question about this. He asks, "Why not do it the easy way? Why not forget about the damn product, and focus on finding groups who already want and buy things they are nutso for.....and just sell them what you know they <u>already</u> want? Why create a challenge? Why create or get products/services and pray you can find people to sell them to? As my friend Dan Kennedy says, 'shoot fish in a barrel with the water drained out.' Challenges are for people who feel good for just overcoming challenges. I feel good getting lots of money the easy way!"

Tapping Into The Power Of TV

Jeff's most recent joint venture, with a top broker of consumer products to the home shopping TV channels, has led to one product (a financial organizer kit) sold on QVC, another in development. As of this writing, over 2-million dollars/70,000 units have been sold solely on QVC. In typical Jeff style, he first appeared on QVC to present the product, but quickly replaced himself with a "hired gun" actress-spokesperson, thus freeing himself from manual labor. Jeff says, "It's nice to sit at home with Peggy, watching the actress sell the product on TV......again making money 'in my underwear'!"

Tapping Into The Power Of Technology

In another joint venture, Jeff has provided his marketing models, for multi-step mailings, follow-up systems, and sales information to a software developer, to produce new, proprietary software to accurately track results, automate and manage all the direct marketing functions of a business. "We built this," Jeff says, "because we couldn't buy it. This is the first and only automated marketing software designed by a marketer."

At the very least, just about every business owner would be well served by investing in a library of Jeff's materials. One good joint venture that results in uncovering hidden profits you didn't know you had can easily recoup the investment a hundred or more times over. But beyond the practical, what-to-do and how-to-do-it contents, there is a great deal to be gained from the attitude and thinking of "the man who knew what he did not want to do."

CONTACT INFORMATION:

Jeff Paul

FAX: 630-778-0019
E-Mail: arguswest@ntsource.com
Website: www.instantprofits.com

* * * * * *

<u>Chapter #9</u>

The Renegade Millionaire

This is the Chapter about me.

I didn't choose that 'Renegade Millionaire' moniker; it was suggested to me by an executive at an infomercial company where I do a lot of consulting. But I kind of like it.

I've made my entire career out of originating or identifying, improving and teaching renegade advertising, marketing and business-building strategies. My monthly 'No B.S. Marketing Letter' emphasizes this each and every month. I'm delighted to tell you that it's one of the most widely read, successful, privately published marketing newsletters in America - and you cannot subscribe to it! You must be a Member of my Inner Circle to receive it, along with other business-building benefits.

I've long operated my own business in a renegade manner. My activities include professional speaking, presenting specialized seminars and 'boot camps', consulting, coaching, and freelance, direct-response copywriting. I may be the least accessible person in any of these businesses in America. For years, we have had our office telephone answered "live" only one designated afternoon each week; all calls to voice mail other times; messages and FAXes dealt with at our convenience. I <u>never</u> take incoming calls, and often deal with clients or client-candidates by pre-scheduled telephone appointments. I do <u>not</u> carry a cell-phone or beeper nor do I personally use e-mail (although we do a considerable amount of business via our web sites). I <u>never</u> have free meetings with companies or individuals contemplating hiring me for consulting or copywriting; each relationship begins with a paid day of consultation. Ironically, I'm a marketing consultant who does no marketing. In my copywriting work, I never accept fees only; my compensation is always fee plus royalties linked to results. I arrange my schedule and affairs for my convenience - for example, on consulting days at my Ohio location, I often start the day at 10:00 AM, so I can spend the first part of the morning at the racetrack, working with our racehorses. Incidentally, we have no employees, and haven't had any for several years, however our publishing/seminar/coaching/consulting business services thousands of Members worldwide, puts on events attended by hundreds, provides on-going coaching, and, in total, produces between a million and two million dollars annually. (I sold my much larger product/mail-order company in 1999).

I tell you that because one of the things I do in coaching is help business owners, sales professionals, etc. realize that they, too, can prosper without trading away their life and sanity; that they can train their customers; that they do not need to (actually, don't even benefit from) ready accessibility; they can take total control of their time; and they can use certain positioning and marketing strategies to make all this possible.

In the speaking profession, I'm also considered a renegade. I've had a very good 20 year career in speaking, including 9 consecutive years on the big SUCCESS events tour, with audiences of 10,000 to 20,000 people per city. Unlike many of my speaking colleagues, I have never sought business from bureaus, do not do "showcases", do not mass mail brochures, have never tele-marketed meeting planners, insist on a non-refundable 50% fee deposit the day an engagement is booked even if it's a year away, and never accept an engagement where I cannot offer my educational materials for sale on site. Also unlike most peers, I rebate a percentage of those sales to the corporate, association or other client, often winding up paying them more than they pay me.

Incidentally, I stuttered uncontrollably as a kid, and nobody would ever have imagined me becoming one of the most successful professional speakers in the business. I have no college education, formal training, apprenticeship or other qualifications in advertising, yet I've become a top advertising copywriter, routinely commanding upwards from $25,000.00 per project - with over 80% of all clients who utilize me once, doing so repeatedly.

With all that said, I thought about what few points I might make in this chapter, in this book, that might be most useful.

Here's one: virtually everything I have wound up doing well, being successful at, and being recognized and respected for, I started out doing very badly, awkwardly and unsuccessfully. Based on my experience, I am absolutely convinced you need no natural talent in order to be wildly successful in a chosen occupation, vocation or business. Entrepreneurs and marketers are definitely made, not born.

Another: just about everything I've figured out how to do successfully through costly and painful trial-and-error, I've subsequently turned into a formulaic process others can use as a valuable shortcut.

Another: if there is a single "secret" to my successes, it is getting things done. Not being smarter or more talented, not even doing things as well as they might be done. Just forcing myself to be what I call a "get done-er".

Finally, I've come to view "marketing" as a means of developing successful businesses that serve their owner's objectives, preferences, financial goals and lifestyle goals.

How My Coaching Programs Work -
And What You Can Learn
About Yourself
Just From Understanding
Why They Work

As of this writing, I have two coaching programs. GoldPlus, limited to 30 Members, provides each member with a 15-minute private, one on one telephone coaching session once a month, ten months out of twelve, group teleconferences the other two months, on top of Gold Inner Circle Membership, which includes the newsletter and monthly audio cassettes. In the 15-minute sessions, we are able to address two to three specific issues with the Members who are well-prepared for their calls.

There is also GoldPlusVIP, again limited to 30 Members. This includes everything in GoldPlus, and three group meetings during the year; mastermind sessions for the group, that I facilitate. (In the months of the meetings, there are no calls.)

What people tell me about the benefits of these programs is that it forces them to be accountable for implementation of ideas and progress from one month to the next, and to focus their thoughts once a month on what they've accomplished and what key marketing challenges they are facing.

While the quality of my advice has value, it seems that what being in the programs compels the people to do for themselves has even greater value. I'm quite certain this is true of the people participating in others' coaching programs as well.

If you don't have a coach, via some other means you definitely need frequent measurement, accountability and assessment, in order to achieve all that you can.

The Coaches' Coach,
The Consultants' Consultant

Quite possibly, my crowning career achievement has been my work as the consultant to America's leading consultants, coach to America's coaches, in many fields.

In dentistry, for example, 'The Successful Practice Newsletter' named me one year as "#1 practice marketing guru", and I'm pleased with the many dentists who've benefited from my methods. But also in that profession, Greg Stanley of Whitehall Management, Linda Miles, and Dr. Bob Willis and Dr. Chris Brady have all been private clients of mine. Dr. Tom Orent is a 2nd-year member of my Gold+ Coaching Program. Their names won't mean anything to you unless you're a dentist. If you are, you know they are all famous, well respected practice consultants in dentistry.

My other private clients who are top consultants in their own right include Joe Polish (profiled elsewhere in this book), Craig Proctor, Jay Mitton and Bill Hammond. Craig Proctor, one of the top five ReMax agents, has a coaching program serving nearly 1,000 real estate agents. Jay Mitton is widely regarded as the father of modern asset protection, and provides asset protection and tax reduction training and coaching to thousands of affluent entrepreneurs and professionals. Bill Hammond is an elder law attorney, specializing in Alzheimer's law, now providing practice marketing training and coaching to hundreds of other attorneys. I could continue this list.

My Platinum Inner Circle is in its 5th year. It is limited to fifteen individuals, all in the information, training, consulting and coaching businesses, each paying dues exceeding $7,000.00 a year to meet and share information, under my direction. Each of my Platinum Members is a very successful consultant in a different, specialized field or niche market, including restaurants, auto repair shops, tax preparation offices, chiropractors, menswear retailers, and so on. Combined, their clientele and coaching program members number more than 50,000 business owners!

Many of these consultants and coaches have businesses generating two million to as much as twenty million dollars a year. Having these extraordinary business leaders continue to turn to me for ideas, information, strategies and direction is, indeed, a privilege.

CONTACT INFORMATION:

Dan Kennedy

FAX 602-269-3113
Website: www.dankennedy.com

* * * * * *

Chapter #10

What Do They Have In Common

I've often pointed out that if, when they were still living, you put Sam Walton and Dave Thomas in a room together, and interviewed them, or just observed them, you'd find many obvious similarities, but if you compare either of them to, say, Donald Trump, or Madonna, or Rupert Murdoch, or Richard Branson, you'd have to look a lot harder to find the similarities - it is the dramatic differences that would be obvious.

Bginning in 1917, with Andrew Carnegie's support, a young writer named Napoleon Hill began a 20 year quest, meeting, interviewing and spending time with hundreds of the greatest inventors, industrialists and entrepreneurs of the time period, from Henry Ford and Thomas Edison to the inventor of the modern, self-serve supermarket. Hill went in search of their shared commonalities of thought, personality, character and behavior. He ultimately identified 17 to write about, in his works *'Laws Of Success', 'Think and Grow Rich', 'Grow Rich With Peace Of Mind'*, and others. Hill's approach has been borrowed and used by a number of authors since, because the value in analyzing successful people is in finding the commonalities. Not what they do differently but what they all do the same.

In this book, you've met eight of today's most successful, unique entrepreneurs who are also in the business of educating, consulting, coaching and motivating others. I know them all well. They are different in hundreds of ways. But there's no value in citing their differences. There is value in citing their commonalities. Here are a few:

These great teachers are committed, aggressive lifelong learners, continually investing their time and money in acquiring new ideas or re-evaluating old ones, in unending search of anything that might improve, even incrementally improve their own ability or results. I can attest to this firsthand, as these people all have spent and spend considerable sums of money with me. Most of them have been or are members of my Platinum Inner Circle. And I know that they are constantly buying and reading new or old but just discovered books, listening to tapes, clipping articles, going to seminars, because they alert me of those I should read, hear, pay attention to. It is always interesting to see them earnestly taking notes at one of my seminars, and thinking that, arguably, of all the people on my list, they may *need* to be there the least. Yet the reason they need to be there the least is that they are always there!

Incidentally, for any of these folks to attend a two day seminar that costs, say, $2,000.00, the $2,000.00 tab is insignificant compared to the value of the time they take away from other activities in order to be there. I would guesstimate the average worth of a day in income if working to the people profiled in this book to be between $10,000.00 and $35,000.00. Attending a 2-day seminar costs them $20,000.00 to $70,000.00.

They are testament to the power and value of lifelong learning. Anyone who is at all "cheap" or penny-pinching about this will never get very far in life. My friend Jim Rohn says you can judge a person's bank account by the size of his library. I've often observed, by the way, that people with tiny bank accounts all have houses with no libraries, but usually have big TV's.

(2)

They are *smart* rule-breakers. I wrote a book *"How To Succeed in Business By Breaking ALL The Rules"*, re-published and available in paperback as *"NO RULES: 21 Lies & Myths About Success."* I have always felt little compulsion to obey rules, generally regarding them as the equivalent of low fences built to keep sheep in a pasture, but of no barrier to a 6'4" human being. The sheep analogy is deliberate. Like me, the people profiled in this book violate a thick catalog of industry norms in their respective fields as well as advertising, marketing, business and routine 'rules.' However, I would make this important point: we all strive to be smart about breaking rules. That means we know what they are, and we learn to succeed with them in many cases before experimenting with alteratives. We master coloring within the lines before painting abstracts. This is quite different from unbridled creativity for creativity's sake, or the kind of ignorant, bull-in-a-china-shop, full speed ahead with no charts or maps approach far too many entrepreneurs indulge in.

(3)

Entrepreneurs, probably by nature, tend not to be very good at, or happy about "detail work." The people profiled here are no exception. Yet they are very systems-oriented. They've discovered ideas are valueless without implementation, and that success without systems is stress and chaos. Every one of these people can show you detailed, thoroughly thought out charts of their marketing processes. Every one of them utilizes a lot of "automated" marketing tools and technology. Every one of them, in fact, has a "system" for making money that works and is replicatable, in much the same way McDonalds has a system for profitable fast food restaurant operation. This is why you can look to any of these people for coaching ad direction, with confidence; they each provide a system.

(4)

They are action-oriented. While most people go home from a seminar or a meeting with notes, these folks have already implemented something before the end of the meeting. They see, they "steal", they do.

In my Platinum group, we meet four times a year, and a goodly portion of each meeting is taken up with each Member showing what they tested or implemented based on discussions at the last meeting, and sharing the results. With most people, with 15 in the room, this'd take about 15 minutes, because truth be told, 95% of the people never do much of anything with what they learn. With this group, it takes 8 hours. I have written an entire book about this, called 'The Ultimate Success Secret.' It is just that. It is so simple. Do something. Now. Today. Everyday. Better yet, get something done. Now not later. Everyday.

(5)

They seek significance, not just success. These are very competitive, very goal-oriented, maybe compulsively goal-oriented individuals who pursue high incomes, wealth and financial independence far beyond ordinary needs, with no apologies for doing so. But rather quietly, certainly without pointing it out to people, they also pursue significance. First of all, these people have made it their business, through evolutionary processes, to help others learn and prosper. In most cases, they might do just as well financially, personally, just doing what they do more, and not teaching at all. They choose to share with those willing to learn. Second, they hold nothing back. Anyone who is willing can acquire from them everything they know, every method they use; literally for the asking.

At whatever the price, their experience is a "blue light special" compared to the cost of acquiring it on your own.

What Should You Do
As A Result Of This Book?

If you are not connected to a coach, a coaching program, a quality source of how-to knowledge and on-going support relevant to your type of business or your life goals, by all means get connected!

There are, incidentally, a number of other such providers, who have adapted my "Magnetic Marketing System" to different niche industries and professions, all listed in my annual Million Dollar Resource Directory, provided free to Inner Circle Members.

* * * * * *

INTERNET DIRECTORY

Coach	Website
Bill Glazer	www.billglazermarketing.com
Chauncey Hutter	www.chaunceyhutter.com
Ron Ipach	www.ronipach.com
Dan Kennedy	www.dankennedy.com
Ron LeGrand	www.SDIWealthInstitute.com www.globalpublishinginc.com
Dr. Barry Lycka	www.cosmeticsx.com
Jeff Paul	www.instantprofits.com www.killercopywriting.com
Joe Polish	www.TheGeniusNetwork.com www.joepolish.com
Stephen Roulac	wwwroulac.com www.roulacplacepropertystrategy.com